BUGS UP CLOSE!

MANTISES UP CLOSE

CAITIE MCANENEY

PowerKiDS press

New York

Published in 2020 by The Rosen Publishing Group, Inc.
29 East 21st Street, New York, NY 10010

First Edition

Editor: Elizabeth Krajnik
Book Design: Michael Flynn

Photo Credits: Cover, p. 1 tea maeklong/Shutterstock.com; p. 5 Lutsenko_Oleksandr/Shutterstock.com; p. 7 Amelia Martin/Shutterstock.com; p. 9 AlexBrown/Shutterstock.com; p. 11 Lubor Zelinka/Shutterstock.com; p. 13 Vince Adam/Shutterstock.com; p. 15 ErgTuna/Shutterstock.com; p. 17 tomoki1970/Shutterstock.com; p. 19 Kristina Postnikova/Shutterstock.com; p. 21 korson/Shutterstock.com; p. 22 SKphotographer/Shutterstock.com.

Library of Congress Cataloging-in-Publication Data

Names: McAneney, Caitie.
Title: Mantises up close / Caitie McAneney.
Description: New York : PowerKids Press, 2020. | Series: Bugs up close! | Includes glossary and index.
Identifiers: ISBN 9781725307940 (pbk.) | ISBN 9781725307964 (library bound) | ISBN 9781725307957 (6 pack)
Subjects: LCSH: Praying mantis--Juvenile literature.
Classification: LCC QL505.9.M35 M39 2020 | DDC 595.7'27--dc23
Manufactured in the United States of America

CPSIA Compliance Information: Batch #CWPK20. For Further Information contact Rosen Publishing, New York, New York at 1-800-237-9932.

CONTENTS

A Bug That Preys

Look closely at a praying mantis. With its huge eyes and long, thin shape, this weird little **insect** looks like it might be an **alien**. Its arms are pulled in close to its body, almost like it's praying. But could it really be **preying**?

From Egg to Adult

A praying mantis starts its life inside an egg. Females lay hundreds of eggs, which **hatch** into baby mantises called nymphs. Nymphs sometimes eat other nymphs. The ones that live grow into adult mantises. Praying mantises don't live very long—only around a year.

Parts of a Mantis

A mantis's body has three main parts: the head, thorax, and abdomen. Mantis heads are small and triangle shaped. Mantises can turn their heads backward! They have two large eyes, three small eyes, and two antennae. Mantises use their antennae to find their way around.

antenna
small eyes
large eye

The thorax is the middle part of a mantis and the abdomen is the back part. A mantis's wings and legs are part of the thorax. A mantis has two front legs, or forelegs; two middle legs; and two hind, or back, legs.

thorax
wing

Many Mantises

There are more than 1,800 species, or kinds, of mantises on Earth. Some are tiny, while others can be 6 inches (15.2 cm) long or longer. Some are bright and colorful. The female orchid mantis looks like an orchid, a kind of flower, to **attract** prey.

Blending In

Other mantises use **camouflage** to hide in plain sight. They're green or brown to **blend** in with the plants around them. Sometimes their bodies are even shaped like leaves or twigs! This helps them creep up on their prey.

Moving Like a Mantis

Praying mantises are master hunters. They stay very still, waiting for prey to come by. They use their strong, quick forelegs to snap up prey, and their **spiked** hind legs hold on to it. After eating prey, a mantis will clean its front legs.

A Mantis's Meal

Mantises are carnivores. That means they're meat eaters. Their prey includes other bugs, such as flies, moths, and crickets. However, some large species will even hunt bigger prey, such as lizards, snakes, birds, and mice. Some mantises will eat each other!

Little Helpers

Mantises can be helpful to people. Farmers and gardeners like mantises because they hunt the pests that eat farmers' crops. Some people find mantises so interesting they keep them as pets! But mantises are always happiest in the wild.

Mantises All Over!

Praying mantises can be found nearly everywhere on Earth, other than very cold places. They live on every continent, or major mass of land, other than Antarctica. They live in many different **habitats**, including forests, rain forests, deserts, grasslands, meadows, and cities.

GLOSSARY

alien: A creature from outer space.

attract: To cause someone or something to be interested in something.

blend: To look like what's around you.

camouflage: Colors or shapes on animals that allow them to blend in with their surroundings.

habitat: The natural home for plants, animals, and other living things.

hatch: To break open or come out of.

insect: A small animal that has six legs and a body formed of three parts and that may have wings.

prey: To hunt another animal for food; also, an animal that is hunted for food.

spiked: Covered in sharp points.

INDEX

WEBSITES

Due to the changing nature of Internet links, PowerKids Press has developed an online list of websites related to the subject of this book. This site is updated regularly. Please use this link to access the list: www.powerkidslinks.com/buc/mantises